ON DREAM STREET

DREAM ON DREAM STREET

Poems by Melanie Almeder

T|P

Tupelo Press
Dorset, Vermont

Copyright

Table of Contents

I. Dreaming Industry

II. Decline of a Century

III. Wind Canticles

For Virginia and Robert Almeder

"I wander all night in my vision."

—Walt Whitman,
"The Sleepers"

I. DREAMING INDUSTRY

They want more
than to be in
your dreams.

—Cornelius Eady
"Insomnia"

Mock Orange

Everything on the tongue goes stunned bird.
Long past the hissy-fit thralls of April,
rashes of phlox, purple thistle snowing a little.
And then, like too much love,
there was altogether too much gardenia
in the huddled yards. The heat in a flick of wind
picked itself up and dragged off,
old dog, into the damp cane fields, bee drone,
sighing, sighing of highway, hawks'cries.
A screen door slammed lightly.
A woman hummed nonsense to herself.
The thousand burnt-orange camellias
bent in rot, long past wisteria,
long past bitter kumquat, past the sweet white ache
of mock orange— it was not God,
but those lithe lord gods themselves,
mocking birds, intoning every other voiced thing
from dirt-slicked limbs of magnolias, until, distracted,
they tipped past the waxed leaves the sun makes silver of;
not God, lord gods; not love, insistence, disregard.

Adam and Eve Chased from Paradise
after Marc Chagall

God gave them Eden, bouquet-thick,
green going greener against its own love of being

and, later, a white angel to chase them out.
Chagall, who loved love, swooned at their mistake,

forgave them, gave them a chicken
to cover their sex, a bride's white headpiece,

and a rudder of light to bear them
into the barren world.

Like God, Chagall could not
leave them alone, gave them such a stream

of blue water to issue forth from—
After all, what could they have done?

How could they know the difference between
that tree, from which sprang knowledge and thus

the history of longing, and God,
whose mind must be the full moon

casting shadow, whose body must be the spine
of rose and forsythia gone full bloom.

Look closer: the pines in the background blackened
when they left, an animal wind picked up

and wept. It carried all the disassociated limbs,
a broken-necked girl, the wide loss

some bodies find in other bodies.
Since then, we have been beautiful and flown.

Ode to *Peterson's Field Guide to Birds*

"There is no reason why we should not trust our increasingly educated eyes."
—*Peterson's Field Guide to Birds*

You are desire; your beloved hidden,
near flight, in the thicket.
You are the will to tally the soon-to-be-dead,
love in a dying climate.
If only they would stop,
in the nearest blue distance,
you insist,
and behave—line up on fence posts,
"roadside silhouettes"—
O for the barn swallow, bob white, and shrike.
O for the sweet satisfaction of stillness and counting.
"Make a lifetime list," you say.

My first bird was a red-eyed loon,
slick, drifting by the dock to gaze at me
before it ducked and the black lake took it under.
That night it cried like an abandoned baby.
It was back the next night keening.
Never did that loon, "kwuck"
like a "bark," never was it "common."
Yes, there were the litanies
of sparrows and purple finches
insisting themselves into the eaves,
the panache of red-winged blackbirds,
the erratics of ashy swallows,
the single eagle ruffling in the breeze,
endless buzzards, the occasional towhee.
Always, though, that one just winging by,

at the edge of sight, unidentifiable.
Dreams feathered and wind-tipped,
bones humming in the throat...

I went once to the Green Mountains,
you in tow, looking for the bird that declared itself,
"Look-ee, up here, it's me,
red-eyed vireo, red-eyed vireo."
The oaks would not give the good bird up.
Before you, I didn't know I was in love
with lesser wading birds in and out of flight.
I was the overfed cat lolling
by the window, the piping plovers
tipping by on their toothpick legs.
They were not "plaintive," I tell you,
they simply peeped like small trucks backing up
and off they went, to the lip of the ocean.

Give me the kiskadee
any day, the cave swallow's flight;
give me a decent antillian palm swift,
the topography of bird scapulars—
the good prayer coming, the good prayer going—
and earnest, earthbound,
beholden to the lesser gods fleeing,
I will say I have seen them.

Elegy for Market Street

"Who thought love but a motion in the mind?"
—*Theodore Roethke, "The Dying Man"*

The moon is a catchall,
        is the ebb from whisper to spit,
dictator of our bellies.

At night it rides over tree limbs
        to play a mean charades.
What was it, loved one

I meant to say, the change spilling,
        the water running over,
the patient animal, regret,

haunting the trees?
        We saw the thin man topple himself
from a roof on Market Street;

we bowed our heads to it, the long history of grief.
        Later a girl on a bicycle pedaled slowly by.
The dusk bloomed furiously.

I dreamt the river swallowed
        a red-eyed keening loon.
Once upon a time, there was an old woman

who carried a rib bone.
        It divined lost children, rain.
As she aged it grew small as a toothpick,

finally it canticled only the wind.
          We eat dinner late again.
I will forget everything.

Night lay on the houses and they dissolved.
          The tick-fat moon
gave back the backbones of roofs,

a doorway, a row of blue spruce.
          I am a boy in a tree; a girl across the street
crouches to steal a tiger lily. I love her.

Country Love Song

I try to think of the cup of a hand,
of legs in a tangle, and not the thistle,

though even it, purpled, spiking away,
wants to be admired, wants to say, whistle

a little for me. O every little thing wants
to be loved, wants to be marked by the cry

that brings desire to it, even blue-eyed fly
to the bloated hiss of death. To love is to be remiss:

the horse alone in the wide flat field nods
its head as if the bridle and bit were missed

or mocked; the cow slung with the unmilked weight
of her tremendous teats shoots a look back over her shoulder

at O lonesome me. I want to say to her need
as if crooning could be enough,

sweet, sweet mama. . .truth be told,
the thousand lisping bees to the milkweeds' honey

terrifies me. When the stink of slurry season
is over and the greened fields are slathered, fecund,

overtall foxgloves tip with the weight of their fruit.
Then I dream a little dream of you

and me, curled like two grubs on the top of a leaf
wind-driven and scudding along the lake's surface.

All night we glide to its blue harbor
and back again. The fattened slack of us

singing o darlin' darlin' darlin'.

Poem for the Man Who Does Not Answer the Phone

It is a good thing I am not on some land spit
rattle snake bit, praying the rings will rouse you,
who refuse to answer the phone. A woman could lose a foot that way,

or an entire precious ankle bone could go to rattlesnake rot.
Alone on that swamp spit, on that lick of land
the sun scorched to bits,

a woman could lose the whole leg waiting.
It is a good thing Orange Lake, that ancient most
sink hole is not on fire and I am calling to say,

one lake breaks into flame and the moon itself goes red,
the fossils of ferns unfurl from their limestone graves
and burn. Darling, I'd say, get out of that bed

and see the reasons to love: the cedars' knees, silvered oak trees,
the paths an apple snail traces, ugly possums, Spanish Moss that needs
nothing but the brine of July air.

It's a good thing you are not answering the phone
and I am calling to tell you I'm bit,
the lake burned

the chickens flew the coop, the cows broke out, the rooster went
pacifist. Get out of bed, I'd say, and hear the entire herd
hoofing away, how the barn lists with their loss.

Dreaming Industry

Just as there's a lapse into near quiet, just as we nod off,
one man has filled the dumpster again
with the debris of a gutted building.

He summons a truck, which grinds
up the lane beside us, engine whining.
Month after month, there is no end to his industry.

There must have been a version of him
just next door since the beginning of time,
hammering or sawing a litany of planks.

One night, near delirium, he mistook the edge of my bed
for a seat and he sat there, head bowed,
the gray plaster of him flaking.

Dear Man, I said, please give it a break—
who among us is not a little alone, a little afraid?
Go home. Trust the sanctity of silence.

To think I once slept so lightly
I snapped awake when I heard the murderer's thought
of the white necks of women

as he drove past on the interstate.
These days when I sleep, I drop deeply
and dream the dreams of industry:

sometimes it is Loon Lake, the last quiet place,
now peopled by bees feeding, beavers,
tree fellers, wood chippers.

Or I dream I am in the crowd
the moment the Arc de Triomphe
is finally raised...

Last night, asleep or awake,
I no longer know, I rose to look out
the window at the usual ruckus

and found all the noise
was large ferns unfurling
beside a lough in Ireland.

In the ways of dreams my father was there
fishing the black depths
when a beast, with massive machineries of teeth

arched up towards him. His heart skipped its beat.
I dug in the peat and in the ways of bogs,
found a spear from the Iron Age.

I cut the throat of that beast.
As my will would have it, in this dream
of industry, my father lives forever.

Desire

I forget you the way someone abandons
a field to the tender wreckage
of milkweed, saw grass, and buckeye butterflies.
I forget you the way purple thistle forgets itself
into its gossamer bits taken skyward by the wind.
Former loves, as peaceful as the long married,
we go drifting through the botanical gardens;
the confederate jasmine's excess pungence trails us.
The words of each plant spill like pebbles from our mouths:
mallow, Cherokee bean, bamboo, hibiscus.
In the butterfly garden a wing-haired opalescence flits.
The lacquered green tree frogs chug
like drain pipes in a small, close house
and it rains. From the gazebo stage,
we stare into a greenly manicured field
(such insistent restraint there).
Like this rain, we could give in
to disorder; like rain, let the disorder of wind take us;
like the field, do what rain asks,
o lie down awhile and be fed.

Moon Variations

"...for what is more beautiful than heaven?"

—*Copernicus*

1. Full Moon, August

Night, the insomniac mother,
tidies the house to arrive around us,

listening for our breath. Damp in sweat and needing,
enunciated by cicadas, we hear

how even the mosquitoes thieve on silence.
How the hibiscus shrinks from the night,

and, in your full-blown light, a lizard becomes a pink translucence,
its blue innards unlikely blossoms.

Beneath you, barred owls howl as the forlorn do.
Beneath you, our hands thrum in the milk light.

Mother of roof spines, you were once slice;
during your thin life, we slept deeply, the whole night,

woke in the heat sighing up from the streets,
all dreamings rubbed clean, and knew nothing

was lost that does not come home.
Even the dead were among us.

No one lacked love. It was as certain
as the wide white plates we ate off of.

2. Waxing Gibbous, February

Filling tick belly,
you are the ache of overflow, tide-spill

into the dry and darkening lip of the yard,
drownings. An old woman picking through

the dump heap that night makes of the neighborhood.
You, the thousand lost languages, stutter

across sleeping bodies. Hand on the fevered brow
of being here, on the ledger sheet,

the impossible tally
of a million horse thieves.

3. Barred Owls Under a July New Moon

Nothing like a blue-black night
for you to bob and chatter, all treetop rancor.

Who needs it, light, when so much thrives fatly on air?
Moonless as the night is, dark as a lake,

ferns off the crumbling bricks luminesce;
the wind lifts the long and longer trusses of Spanish moss;

small white delicacies mumble across a field
(green as green cud in its other incarnation, noon light.)

Loud ones, I cannot sleep; I grow less fleshed,
a skin one could step from.

I hear you chat up the prey. I hear them scatter.
Even the rust of lesser moths,

even the magnolia blossoms wide as white cups,
all machinations for devourings.

4. The Moon's Soliloquy

You have had your say and then some,
looking up and looking down human literati.

I have seen the blood you spilled
and still, among you people,

more than previous centuries could have imagined,
tender conclusions:

the good thrum of your own blood pulse,
the sleeping face as quiet as paper beside you.

And this: the book any cast of light makes you into.
The way your voice leaves you,

hovers in your garden, humming.
What was it your hands have done?

You are, after all, in a glance, finished.
Enough, then, of your mean little waltzes

in the name of immortality.
You have been foolish and prophetic

as frogs before a storm when the wind blows back
the silvered underbelly of leaf.

The Old Lie

In Memoriam, Wilfred Owen

He might be any body, loved by his mother,
made fodder to a yellow waste of marigolds.

After all, we have grown weary
of histories that happened in spite of him,

the odorless dead in their trenches, the unrecoverable
sentiences. Of what testament then are the photographs of him

in uniform standing before the doorways
draped in yellow roses, red roses, wisteria,

or the fragmented accounts of those who thought
they saw him last on the bank of the Sambre Canal?

One man claimed Owen patted him on the back, muttered comfort.
Another claimed it rained mud; he saw nothing; heard the bridge snap.

If someone could recall a body from the edge of oblivion,
from the disembodiment numbing history,

it would be only as if we were the man beside him,
the first time his mind was undone, in Etretat—

they were going to take the town; they were close enough
to see the church of the town, to see, even

the sun making the leaves of its trees burn whitely;
and, while the entire ground beneath them splintered,

he saw the church's simple door,
the possibility of the door opening.

Lonely

A ladder on a limb, not even wind
among green leaves. A tin can, rust-lipped

on a steam grate. A bag caught in a bare tree.
Wires. Stand of evergreens. Snow.

The furnace clicking on in the deep of the night.
A buzzard tree ruffling in the breeze. Mole shuffle.

Bullfrog quiet in the pickerel weed.
Street turning onto empty street.

A lover, woken, saying, "I am asleep."
A highway sighing all day long.

A bleating sheep. The dropped key;
the tongue as it meets the back of the teeth.

You, you and me. A beloved body gone
and whom, whom, to tell it to?

Rosary beads hung on the bed post.
Mary, dear Mary. Her white lily.

Somewhere, a child dreams fitfully.
A mother locks the windows, shuts off the lights.

There's a cough at the end of a hospital corridor.
A dock on a lake. A gutted fish. A hook.

A spoon. The moon. A bone.

God in thought on his golden road.

II. DECLINE OF A CENTURY

"I have gone out to look
for a black dog
who answers to my whistle."

—Charles Simic
"Empire of Dreams"

Dumb Luck

after Nicholas Rescher's *Luck: The Brilliant Randomness of Everyday Life*

O the requiems we've sung
to near misses: the rusty nail

clipping the flesh closest
to an artery, the bad oyster

the belly refused, the heart beat
that mis-fired and left the body

breathless. Is it any comfort
that some poor sot

was not favored
the way we were; we side-step

while he trips, is lassoed, is shot,
or meanders cow-like, into death's slick ditch.

Luck was never moral:
there was the man who meant to kill his mother

over a few dollars, doused her
in kerosene, but, try as he might,

the match book was old,
the match would not catch.

She wandered her unholy body
into a street full of traffic and starlings.

Then the good man who ran, hero-like,
into a burning building

but dropped the child on the way out.
The hit-and-runs. The few inches

we have shy of blindness. Right now,
someone, somewhere, who looks an awful lot like us

gets lost in the woods, finds his way home
or does not, lands a white-collar job.

In luck's long history, we fell from a tree;
a feathered thing once interceded on our behalf;

a rattlesnake stuck its spiny fangs
in an ankle bone while we looked on stunned;

once we lost love; once a friend died;
once we almost arrived home in time

to meet the armed thieves, but didn't.
And lucky dogs we were,

lady luck on our arm, luck-of-the-draw,
like the unexpected kiss,

multiplying among us—o love den
of luck, we were our own one-in-a-million-statistic.

The story after luck's demise:
survival is as certain as eating an egg

or not eating it, as easy as a lake is easy,
your own breath your own sweet breath.

Pastoral for a Sad River

Hours from the idea of a delta,
no more than brown thread
in the bottom of the valley's green bowl—
but not lonely; the river spoons the banks
beside the coal cars. On the rare days
when all the trains are west loading
or east groaning on their oiled haunches,
the gutted mountain glistens blackly in their metal beds,
the river utters counterpoint
to the latticed time of empty tracks.

If the river has a source, it is seepage
from the mountains' winters, what is left
after the soil eats its want,
and the pine spears, and the debris speckling the banks.
There are waters busy enough
in their shallow brevity
to be called brills or runnels;
there are rivers that make of granite hefts,
marble eggs; rivers that lift sand coarse as seed
into fumes, but not here.

Six mallards do not care,
lay nests in the weeds and chug against the current,
ticking skinny minnows up.
A kingfisher lays claim to the telephone wire.
One great blue heron barks as it wheels in,
then stares, stock-still, wills trout
where the water meets the bridge abutment.
In March, a pair of hooded mergansers on their way south

stop to rest. They pedal the ochre shallows.
grunt from beneath their fruffed mohawks.

One man we have never seen has made a dock
the size of a small table for his red canoe,
a white plastic carnation at its helm.
One woman each dusk hurls husks of dry bread to the mallards.
The keepers of green space, the cultivators,
have paved a walkway for us,
have staked the crepe myrtles
In spring a rash of yellow daffodils
raises their yellow mouths to the first ache of sun
until the rain undoes them.

Then the water turns the color of burnt sugar
and the wrens and jays pick the banks' grasses for bedding.
The dying man comes here
leaning into his cane, his sister on his arm.
A man and his boy come to fish the small depths.
When we have walked the length of it
and have returned to our warm homes,
shut off the lights, curled to sleep,
we cannot hear our simple river. We cannot hear
the birds all dawn declare it worthy.

Lovers above the Town

after Marc Chagall

This must happen while they are sleeping,
 where wind happens and strange perfection.

He holds her the way
he'd hold the beloved book

he'd read until he was an old man.
Her arm that reaches out to him day after day,

the reach that allows a mother,
that allows gratitude, that allows the infinitude of cosmos,

her one arm reaches toward the unencumbered distance;
it is the bough of their direction.

This, then, is how lovers in their sleep fly
above the town. They are neither sad nor happy.

All night they are immortal
in their tangle of legs.

Beneath them, the city is as city does.
But for one black goat hunched in the snow.

One red building. And one yellow house
from which an abundance of corners springs.

The lovers are the other architecture,
sprung from the town that does not anchor their good bodies

to a bed. They need only two arms,
two legs, two heads.

They are the cradling
at the center of the world

They are their own
unlikely dream of the city.

A Brute Given

"… our wind knocked out of us, we the labyrinths, the ladders,
the trampled spaces…"

—*Hélène Cixous*

O vessel I restlessly occupy,
the long since fallen from grace,

access to touch, to aftertaste
on a tongue, to murder,

remember when the day's bravery amounted
to dressing to the ankles, tucking the hair under a cap

and heading to the edge of the highway to take in the day's
minimal crow life, a winging towhee, to bring oneself home

the non-statistic, to be the not-murdered, the safe kept safe for now?
All of that storied flummery about visitations —southern ladies

ghosted in white by the water oaks at the edge of the graveyard
waiting to tell us who killed them —

was just keening lip service, old wish to catch that body
on the run; I keep dreaming it bangs like a white dove

against the jailhouse's painted window, convinced by a blue tint
that looks like home; surely there was a time,

saint-like, body slipped the chain gang
of anyone frothing at the mouth to have their hands on it,

to finger it, and there it went,
thread-like into the palm hammock

indistinguishable from spider web or frond;
it was then aesthetics wed death;

we have always walked in what was always just beyond us,
iffy soma, mouthing our lullaby,

our own heart-beats in this over-paved landscape
which on a rare day hushes rig-like back at us, "there now, there now."

Four Cures

Cure #1: If You Live in Georgia and You Think God
Spoke Directly to You
       (for Howard Finster)

Listen. Give up your day job:
lay your lawnmower repair tools gently in the cement.

With a stick, scratch the date God said, *Be an artist.*
Paint as many angels as time allows on all the junk

from all the junkyards in town. Bring home broken down lamps,
smashed-up cars. Stack them. Name your backyard 'Eden.'

And when your bones begin to ache, and when death
starts its slow saunter towards you,

hew your own white coffin. Tell your long-bewildered wife
the palette and brushes are hers, as are any remaining heavens.

Cure #2: If Your Love Has Left

Find an egg a hen laid and left.
Cradle it in your palm. Write your beloved's name
over the entire shell. Do not let the shell break.

Find a body of water. It must run.
No lakes. No ponds. Stand facing away.
Toss that well-inked egg over your shoulder.

Listen for the way it breaks
the skin of the water,
the current eating it whole.

You know how this story goes:
do not look back. Walk straight home.
After that, be sensible.

Cure #3: If You Are Bored To Distraction

Put one penny under your tongue.
The whole day, hum

I will outlive my worry.
Watch out what you wish for.

At dusk, when the penny
has made your mouth taste of rust,

when the wind has stilled,
walk to the nearest train track.

Place the penny on the rail. Wait.
The earth will shake:

a train will come and flatten it.
Carry it, useless coinage, to your grave.

Cure #4: If the Roof of Your Home by Sad Chance is Chosen by
Buzzards As a Roost

Cancel paper delivery immediately—
they will only beat you to it, eat the news.

Install a sprinkler system on your roof.
Then string wires all across it.

More than likely they simply will feast
on the neighbors' papers, will strut among your rooftop wires

and pluck them. The twang will keep you from your sleep.
Buzzards adjust better than the rest of us. They will preen

in the rooftop rains. Your ceiling will begin to leak.
Forget the buckets. Give it at most one week. Move.

Women Made of Words

"What should we be without the sexual myth,
the human revery or poem of death?"
—*Wallace Stevens*

Gone, the frothy winds the lustful are spun in.
Gone the priests culling the would-be sex of virgins.

The carnal centuries wore the ears of confessors
to the smoothness of old conchs; now all the specific sins

are one long sound of wind in the drain pipe.
No more breath-bearing Venus, lifting the white spume

to a picked-clean blueness, no buffed and fragrant
and damp goddess, oversexed and benign among us,

perfumed by hibiscus and peppery sea rose and salt as light as aftertaste.
No more, the torturers: without the sexual myth, they transmogrify

into window cleaners, buffing simulacra of cloud migration.
And then sex withers, drops off like Morning Glory blossoms.

Off drops Helen of Troy, Troy, Carthage.
Gone the begotten trench, the bloody stump, pulcritudes of land

bombed into a pocked birdlessness. Imagine God walking
in the shade of the day and no nakedness to intuit.

Imagine the litany of rapes in the forms of swans and golden rains,
the historic fatigue of them, dissipating.

And a "Song of Solomon" bare and numb as anesthetic sleep;
where the beloved does not intone, find him,

among myrrh and fig and frankincense, find him,
tell him, I have grown tired of love.

Decline of a Century

Still there were the waxed calendulas,
the red-tipped hibiscus, the peace roses, pink

unto unreal whiteness, and there were the usual
unruly bees, the stinks of honeysuckle, the occasional

throaty purr of humming bird.
Nearby, a town made tinder by July burned

like a determined, steady thought.
Ashes sighed up the sky. Within spitting distance,

the Cafe Risque sold "life-like erotic parts"
and promised "bare-all buffets." The mother around the corner

found one of the sex toy discards, mistook it
for a dismembered woman, called the sheriff, parted the bougainvillea,

"to find the rest of the poor girl." Tenderness had a time of it,
sighed like the unholy heat, and then slid by us.

It was our golden fish, gone back to quiet depths.
The sun burned bone-white.

We stared clouds into a familiar face,
the day into a fact, like a kiss.

La Pluie

after Marc Chagall

In the stillness of the yard, a headstone,
its lists of ancestors obscured
by wind and dirt, by black shadow
and in the foreground a woman falls
as she runs for the house;
her hand reaches out to her husband,

who does not see her—
who descends the stairs
with an umbrella in his hand,
all of him a posture of purpose;
all of him headed in the other direction, to town.
She falls; she is the same grey
as the sky, as the ground, the clouds

about to break. The farm's roofline is stitched
as if by children, with red yarn.
The horse in the open barn door,
Its fear domesticated, hoof and bit;
though it stand stock-still,

its ears flick; its eyes are spooked
wide. On the blackened hill above the barn,
a man is so angry, the rooftops seem to pitch
below him. His whole body rises
and leans into the whip. You want to say,
you say, O, see, he's trying to herd a goat,

an impossible goat—
but you know, you know, this is ancient,

unending rage, the coming rain an excuse
for his full weight into the lash of the whip.
The goat's white head twists back,
as pain does, towards torture's insistence.

The only green thing: the tree at the center,
bent by the pull of wind in the frail sails of its blossoms.

Ode to an Egg

for Don and Galen

1.

One way or another,
the world that birthed
the chicken birthed you.
Sweet inevitability,
you dropped, split open
and the yolk of an earth
yellowed our mouths.
Since then, dear stone
with a heartbeat,
centuries flipped you,
willed you whipped,
souffléd, the shine
on the meat, the puff in the pastry,
over hard, over easy.
Alone with our dawn thoughts,
the morning sun bleeding
along rooftops, we spoon
your innards as if they were
a delicate soup in its spoon split cup.

2.

The overfed chef
sleeps uneasily, dreams his hand
plucks rocks from nests, then tosses them
through his meat-eating neighbors' windows.
Startled, they raise
their faces, their bloody maws,
to gaze through the splintered panes

out at a dark night they cannot fathom.
Then he dreams his wife's
hair is a nest, a lair,
he some Thom Thumb of food
sweetly ensnared.
But the perfumed grasses of it
harden into snakes
snap, snapping towards
the red defiant egg
of his heart.

3.

Dear egg, when you were
lost to us,
whether by wind or water
or larger human slaughters;
when you stayed tucked away
in a grotto of leaves, ungathered,
you took your fine time,
forging a heart and lung,
a crook of a leg,
a fuzzed skin,
a slick and feathered thing
to peck through one thin world
into the wide life of bodies,
feathers, cloud rub, the blued
and bluing skies,
pebbles and grammars envied you.

On Dream Street

after W. Eugene Smith

"Dream Street" tilts against its own axis,
points to the curve, then to the end of the world.

Day left its husk of light to the huddled maple trees.
Now it is always dusk; otherwise, aloneness—

an old Ford parked off the edge of a curb,
the road turned back into thickets.

The houses put away like plates
onto the dark shelves of their being.

The street hums with a lullaby
we've sung about the river drying up,

the shard case of its bottom
sifted by an ancient mud-eyed turtle

wide as a moon; the black muck and slick of leaves
beneath him. On Dream Street need was a fine

and feathered thing we gathered up,
carried home to feed.

I was the truant girl chasing sleep.
I was a catch in the throat of loneliness.

Now, the creak in the trees when the wind rides
through them. Now the field a riot of seed.

For Silence

If only grief could suckle silence and like a milk-filled baby,
drop off the nipple of its white absence into a sleep simple and deep.
What we would do, wouldn't we, to hold a body against collapse

or will it, unbroken, back. Breath after breath we'd give
to swim the world of the beloved dead, to pull them
toward the clean horizon of a story we'd sing.

Silence, unresentful vessel toward which the world empties,
take us. Make sense of us. After the verbiage passes,
make us the old wordless verb of being.

In our small history, we built tunnels,
and when we came upon a river, canals. And after sky
upon sky, we built high rises. We loved the bone homes

our bodies made. We fattened cities; we fled them.
It is true: an entire century startled, went still.
The trenches we leave will fill with a quiet, mindless rain.

From the Front Door to the Mailbox and Back

I.

I think I'll get my hair trimmed today.
I'll emphasize that the pictures in the book won't do:
no to razor-cut plumes, no
to tinted, multilayered wedges. Something simple.
Tucks and curls. Bangs to arch above my eyebrows.
Tendrils to trail the nape of my neck. Yes, the subtle
Nefertiti look will be fine, I'll say.
Let the hair bespeak allure so I may rise
a coifed queen of sorts and swank back,
the obvious mistress of my home.

II.

Eddy, the stray cat who stayed, blinks
from his armchair perch at the window, at me,
at the pile of teacups, china plates, saucepans,
I've heaped like relics
in the center of the living-room floor.

The saucepans make a winging sound and then
a dull thunk when they hit the wall,
nicking it. Several have thunked
then toppled across the floor. Teacups don't smash
the way you'd think: to bits, or folding in on themselves.
They split. Or crack. They are sturdier
than they look. Almost even-tempered.
China plates splinter entirely, like relief,
and ring a sound close to wind chime.

I'm not really angry;
It's just that last night I thought
what what what
and from an ocean pool
in my sleep, a blue whale
hunched up backwards and beached himself.
The way an avid bird watcher would exclaim
"red-eyed vireo, red-eyed vireo," I hollered
"it's a blue whale, a blue whale"
and bent over him. His belly was white
as tenderness. I listened for his breath.
He was talking to me.
I can't remember what he said
but it sounded like my aunts muttering
lovingly over meals.

III.

Lakota tell a story:
there's an old woman always somewhere
threading a blanket with porcupine quills.
The same black dog licks and licks
his paws and never breaks his gaze from her.
A pot of sweet berry soup brews footsteps away.
It must be stirred. Just as she leaves the stitching
and stirs, the dog pulls out the quills
and the blanket falls to pieces. She returns
and resumes. It goes on and on.

If she ever finishes
the blanket, this world will end.
It's not the same story as the world
on an oak post chewed at by a chipmunk.

The world here isn't round or flat.
This world isn't inevitable ending
and she's no moping Eve, either.
She's no Pandora
who's picked up a few good tricks.
The hag tucks quills,
disregards the hound, never sips the soup.
She's old: she knows a thing or two.

III. THE WIND CANTICLES

We can tell whether we are happy by the sound of the wind. It warns the unhappy man of the fragility of his house, hounding him from shallow sleep and violent dreams. To the happy man it is the song of protectedness: its furious howling concedes that it has power over him no longer.

—Theodore Adorno
Minima Moralia

Elegy, Key West

Blue fricatives persist. Old parrot calls. The yellowed moon.
Long gone, the lonely madness of the lighthouse keeper,
the bone-snap of limbs in a hurricane.
The railroad and its long want, Audubon, his bags of pretty birds:

to wind and water, to time. Still the mackerel, the silver spit
of tarpon, the blue tang. Long gone the wreckers' wish
for the sinking ship and the first one there pilfering
pianos from the blue churn. Somewhere deep, the broken hull of a boat

spills its innards in a tide pull. Gone the pirates
and their hangman. Still the hangman's tree. Still the bone urns
in the cemetery; the drunks losing their keys. Gone
Hemingway. In his shadow, the big-toed cats breed.

Gone Bishop. Gone Capote. An old boat captain
who drowses under the shade of a mimosa tree
and dreams the one place in all the seas where sharks sleep
in currents riffling over them, their gills as quiet as napkins.

A few burrowing owls, a few thickets of lime.
The fatness of heat and of time, of frondescence. The sun burning
everything to the same bone-white.
Still the blue begetting blue, still the wind soon to rise.

Resurrection City

I loved an entire town where brimming-over
ocean met swamp met subterranean limestone.
Day after day on the sole highway,

armadillos startled into the grills of a hundred
cars and never learned any differently.
The funeral men had long since moved north,

to firmer earth. The dead in their caskets
couldn't be moored; each first hurricane,
up they'd come; the wind would drive them

toward a fine line of blue horizon.
The place should have been training ground
for penitents: the shallows bred razor-sharp shoals;

town officials sprayed Malathion
to kill the innumerable mosquitos.
The poison stained our white t-shirts.

Billions of hungry barnacle mouths
snapping open when the tide slid in.
And just beneath that that curve of Gulf bay,

the bottom-crawler catfish, all scud and sludge
and slow moving eyeballs.
The shrimp boats with their uptucked nets

charged home every dusk,
buzzed by bucket-chinned pelicans,
stink of salt flesh abundant;

their motors announced, night is coming,
night is coming. And on those cusps, dusk was like forgiveness.
The brackish back-water stilled to a stew.

Dragonflies, oblivious to the rot smell
of cottonmouths, oblivious to the alligators which,
if they could pray, would pray for poodles,

did high-tech gymnastic balance acts
on water stained by tannin, the blood rust
leakage of cypress trees.

Their skinny swatches of iridescent green,
their wings like fragile lace, set you aching.
A place like that made you stare into the sky and wait.

The Wind Canticles

1. Emissary

Two black crows strut
through the fine unmown
green. The pines shrug
their boughs. A chime
tosses in the wind like a buoy
on an angry sea. And so
the ocean tosses its baskets
of blue silks, the white threads
of all the hems undone.
My love is sad.
Not from gravity, from the way
it pulls at his face and forges
tender rivulets of age.
His eyes look out *sadly*
as he said of his own father,
sadly at me. The wind tosses
its buckets of breath.

2. Nocturne: Biddeford, Maine

Crisp and salted. Smear
of factory, smear of paper
in the air. And streetlights,
engines in their small guttural hums.
At the beachside bar, fishermen
in the amber light; smoke fumes
muting them. Farther out in the dark,
like some grand cow bell
of the ancients, a buoy
wind-tossed saying here,
here. I wanted that night blueness,
to be its shell well-salted,
its sleeping mouth.
Intake and sigh.
The slow deep shrug of tide.

3. Nocturne: Hermit, Manana Island

The muscled gulls careen and mewl.
Beneath them, infinity of sea,
bloodworm, brine, spiny fish.
On the field above sheep bleet,
scatter, settle to cud green.
We are here to eat and be eaten.
Rogue ocean, blue grave,
the only ghost I know is the wind
through everything. Once I thought it was
my mother's voice humming
honey dear, honey dear,
as if I were a life
in a bone and driftwood cradle,
as if there were something more
and it did not love or mind us.

Migratory

All July, two bored boys broke and broke
the tender necks of grass snakes;
now a murder of crows shags the magnolias black,

rouses the air with a clamor
incessant as hounds loosed after the hunted.
The body intoned no more than the unending leave-taking

any highway breathes: the dead, simply, left.
And if all the broken ones do come back
in summer going rust to visit our sleeping bodies,

they do not whisper the counterfactual or comfort;
the girl refuses to be written the *always*
the flush of youth; she remains loosed

in the burning house, in the dark and blooming air.
The suicide mutely refutes regret, merely stares,
the last taste of air in his mouth.

We will arrive into the hush of winter,
the thick breath of home, and an oblivion of summer lakes
in our dreamings, frail golden leaves falling from the ceilings,

a thousand blue-black swallows suturing the dusk.
Then the quick rush of snow off the roof will wake us,
will loosen night into that other whiteness

of street lights and damp flakes,
spinning with the endless benignity of gnats.

Hermeneutics of Lust

O rattlebox tethered to a corset of ribs, touch once sent the light into a stutter. You: other, beloved, prophet of sweat and frond, stepped from a pool of shade. The water oaks indicated infinity. Our bodies arched into hills. The history of your parted lips: salt on tongue tip, the pale want of you when you slept. A tribe of dreams scattered across your face. All the while, tenderness cut deals with monuments and tears. When you left, the runway models, their opiate pupils fixed on nothing, their androgynous teeth set in a clench, sauntered right down the center of the bombed century, draped in some retro-fathers-of-the-deserts-frocks. They spun on perfect heels, gave a hip twitch, and then drifted back towards that black curtain of emergence, their hunger immortal.

Ode to Borrowed Time

There's no getting back to where purity breeds
in the mouths of saints but summer tries its best—
the way sidewalks keep steady time, birds break the air,
and on some summer days, grackles settle
into the wide pines, their sounds,
a thousand frying pans, their leaving, one black breath.

There are mornings the light is an invalid.
What happened years ago,
what happened yesterday, becomes a speak,
a say, dust sashaying. What happened while we slept,
an absenteeism, throat bones humming their song.
In the night, what is left: the attics of our breath.

The house was my mother's dreaming,
the chimney, a reed; the finches, yellow insistence.
Here a man kissed the hard board of my back
and it softened. We could raise our hands
to hear the light's annunciation
pool in the teacups and basins: the trees will marry
the wind, we will beget ourselves all over again.

House of Gris-Gris

for Betye and Alison Saar

Gods wrought from discards:
Venus of rusted nails, her heart, glass shards.
Her entourage: Lazarus rising from the mouth of a junkyard dog,
a rooted woman pocked with flesh wounds;
a man, his hands on fire, his face a welded acquiescence.
As much as they are metal, are wood found and wrought,
they are all half-done, caught. The face of Venus
opens into: "The House of Ancient Memory,"
small as a shoe box, filled with mano azul,
the pink fatigue of crepe-paper over crepe-paper.
You could pick it up, carry it home through the Georgia heat.
You could carry it home the way you carry a long bouquet.

But the yard they're caught in waits
the way the house at the end of the room waits:
someone has swept a path, someone has opened the gate.
Beaded bonitas dance a mamba mambo in a wake of buttons.
A lion eats a sunflower. A cedar bottle-tree speaks
some other tongue of lights. Then—the way your coat waits—
the tin wings hang there for you to step into them.
The door of "The House of Gris-Gris" has been half-opened,
a man of wood is asleep on its stoop. Someone has named him
"Sweet Dreams." You could step over him
into the dim recesses, but his face is a door.
You could reach toward him. You could open him—
the way you would open an oven or a cellar—
and you would find only the wide night, its bric-a-brac of starlight.

Palm Hammock

Dusk, the insistent cicada,
the soul that like the open-mouthed whip-poor-will
flies and gorges on the brine life of small wings.

All night golden orb spiders lace curtains
between water oak limbs, then they climb them
skyward, and perch.

On rare dawns, wind tips ragweed,
tips the drowsed heads of sunflowers.
The world goes unkempt.

It needs endless tending.
The wide hush beneath the underbelly of leaves:
Sweet Gum, Saw Palmetto, Sumac, White Ash…

Zebra Longwing drifts to rest on thistle tip.
O edged and evanescent,
let the dry rub of palm frond be the old song of making song.

Florida Pastoral

Late July rage gave way,
lack chatted up the heat,
bumble bees slipped in
and out of hibiscus blooms,
riling them. Limes greened
against the parch of late day.
Night after night could not
keep out scintillates of starlight,
the dizzy grief of light-seeking
moths, the perfume of Dixie
Orange blossoms riding in
on a faint May wind,
the house littered for a week
with hitched-at-the-hips
love bugs. One morning, a gray
wolf spider sensed us in the bed,

stopped her scurry across the floor,
wobbled her eye stalks.
We knew that after days
we would become that buzzard tree
shuffling its black and greasy feathers;
Spanish moss dropping its dry tresses
down the length of us. Our bodies,
the ladder the lizard craved,
the quick roost of humming birds honed
for the honeys of reds.
Our mouths, buds; our tongues,
iffy pollen-slicked stamen.
Mad state, it was true,
love made the body a bit frond,

a bit of pink lizard. Dusk after dusk,
the big-bellied orange moon sashayed up the sky,
not a blooming thing sleeping.

Water Histories

1. Oswego

for Lisa

Once we lived in a town where alewives
beached themselves every spring.

People lived through winters as white and sooty
as the one before, as the one after.

They waded in the snow;
they made wide sounds.

Fallsbrook was the orange river;
muddied periwinkles pearled the edges.

A ruby water snake cut a quiet swath
across its mirror stillness. Oswego returns

the way a hummingbird does, a purred insistence
tacking in, away: then the sugar water yellows

and the ice floes begin their humming
like a loosening thought.

2. Rangeley

At the lip of Loon Lake, glint
of mica in the sand; the wide eggs of granite,

minnow flit, old smell
of gutted trout off the dock, a wind

knocking the boats against wood, rustling
up a grackle from the bed of pearly everlastings,

a wind and the long thought
of clouds on the lake top goes skittering;

we are in the muscled belly of daylight.
Dog barking, barking in the distance.

The smell of the lake: damp leaves
in a darkness. Hummingbirds

to the dusty yellow mouths of tiger lilies.
Such hovering. The hum of a thousand bees

from beyond the birch trees. Once, a white sturgeon
rising up from the blacker depths to die:

old dinosaur, mud-eyed. Quiet bubbles from his mouth.
The whole ache of August made him bone.

More lovely than the water lily's
white cups: their swampy underbellies, the suck

of their roots breaking up from the muck.
Bear at the road curve, fat blueberries smeared on her maw.

The old she-racoon we fed, her eyes flashing red;
late, when everyone sleeps, the loon keens,

keens; Saddleback Mountain wings her cry
back to the cupped lake, to the small house crouched there,
the soundings seed our small bodies becoming.

Lowell Sonnets

1.

The town was an architecture of absenteeism,
dimming lineage in the ash light of March.
Lowell, the reliquary of family.
There, she should have been birthed holy entity;
but our beloved, in the yards of the white
quietudes of Mary, refused her own
emptying, grew irrefutably.

Lowell became our gristle, our whiskey,
all that insists: sweat, roilings in the gut,
fecund gone gone late
blood-rust lilac blossom.
Brushing against it we feared what flesh
promised in the sweet decay of exude:
we will be eaten into a bone solitude.

2. Postmortem

Lowell's gone ash can, gone soot, gone hybrid
of lilac and factory and lapsed Catholic.
Leaves, the disoriented speak of trees;
with a little wind, they talk the shuffle, the sweep.
At night strange resemblances among teeth and grave stones:
We've got heads full of relatives
while the wind trills the silver ash leaves.

In the story of the city,
in the old woman's grin back
at the wind and blue sky, teeth are the spokesmen
of bone, would have, if they could have, told
the one about skeleton where skin
makes off with the crows, wind pilfers sockets,
and later, much later, the bureaucracy of souls.

A Dance for Lillian Who Loved Her God

for Lillian Sullivan

In the fat-lipped month of May, mud-honeyed, evening burrs
with black flies and purple finches.

The Atlantic mutters up a waste of delicate skeletons.
We try to comfort ourselves: there will be room enough

for your death, for ashen fogs making salt slicks of our skin,
for the Northeasters that bring wind keening into the eaves.

Our pulses will count us into night, into daylight.
Then the angels of afterthought, grown large,

will spin into superstitions: we will set an extra plate for you.
All of June will be a blue-grey thicket of tides.

Who, after the habit of forgetting that is living
could conjure the exact angle of her eyes?

We gave over to something in this place then,
some hybrid of wish and blood thrum, some will to suffice.
The light warmed up its instruments, played the first chord.

Elegy for Grief

It is the come home to roost, grief,
which, unattended, settles in,
mundane as furniture.
What, after all, are we to do with it?
This sweet old world cannot bear grief
along for long, either:
like industry, like lapse,
like light gone slack into the edge of dusk
before the black oblivion of night:
the world lingers on its objects and insists,
in any loss, on some loveliness.

Who were we to imagine immortality?
The death of aesthetics ?
Napoleon himself needed a nap.
Our best theatrics, the gods, our losses,
refuse to punish us,
but loll among us, abstracted
into other mild states resembling the play of light.
And in this, loved one,
the one I thought the trees lay their leaves down for once,

you are no more than the abandoned instrument
in the forgotten ballroom of the gods.
You are no more than the window there
open to endless kudzu. You are no more
than the crumbling limb of a marble statue, than the pink light
against which swallows stitch untranslatable erratics.

Verge

The landscape prayed its litany
of dusk, grieved us, did not need us.

Daylight grew fat, grew slack with fatigue;
the pond scum thickened.

If you listened, the limestone sunk beneath
your tired feet told you

you were water before you were flesh,
and wind before that.

Your bones may leave a fine shape, like old fish,
like curved shells; we happen

the way light happens:
after the thunderstorms ride the sky,

day's skin darkens. Beneath it, a hawk
quiets. Pink lizards skirt the window light

and the Luna Moth bangs like an amnesiac angel
against the screen. Later sleep will weave

the wet through our ribs; we will grow wide,
slatted, unmoored, born by tide-heave of dreaming,

o body, old boat of time and breath, no less, no less.

Acknowledgments

Poetry   "Country Love Song"

Iron Horse Literary Review   "Pastoral for a Sad River"
                                            "Dumb Luck"

Georgia Review   "From the Front Door to the Mailbox and Back"

The Seneca Review   "Elegy for Market Street."
                                            "Ode to Peterson's *Field Guide to Birds*"

Five Points   "Mock Orange"

Southern Poetry Review   "Desire"

The American Literary Review   "The Old Lie"
                                            "The End of Grief"

Mississippi Review   "Hermeneutics of Lust"

Comstock Review   "Poem for the Man Who Does Not
                                              Answer the Phone"
                                            "Lovers Above the Town"

flyway   "A Brute Given"

The Minnesota Review   "Decline of a Century"

Margie   "Lonely"
                                             "Dreaming Industry"

32 Poems   "For Silence"
                                            "The Lowell Sonnets"
                                            "Verge"

Diner   "Adam and Eve Chased from Paradise"
                                            (as "Adam and Eve Chassis")

The Cortland Review   "Four Cures"

Connotations   *"Moon Variations"**
                                            "Water Histories"
                                            "Ode to an Egg"

*A musical setting of "Moon Variations" for soprano, clarinet and piano, was composed by Gordon Marsh in 2001, and first performed April 2001, featuring Marianne Sandborg, soprano; Colleen Hartun, clarinet; and Gordon Marsh, pianist.

Thank you to Debora Greger, Jeffrey Greene, John Poch, Keith Cartwright, Karen Duddy, and Giuliana Chapman for your fine writing, insight, and generosity at all stages of this work. Thanks to Channing Johnson for all of your help. The community and writing time these institutions provided was invaluable: Tyrone Guthrie Centre, The Woodstock Guild (especially Katherine Burger), The Island Institute of Alaska, The Faculty Development Committee, and the AWP Writer's Conference Award.

Special thanks to Jeffrey Levine, Margaret Donovan, and the Tupelo Staff.